GRAPHING AND PROBABILITY WORD PROBLEMS: NO PROBLEM!

MATH BUSTERS WORD PROBLEMS

Rebecca Wingard-Nelson

NEED MORE PRACTICE?
free worksheets available at
http://www.enslow.com

Enslow Publishers, Inc.
40 Industrial Road
Box 398
Berkeley Heights, NJ 07922
USA

http://www.enslow.com

Copyright © 2011 by Enslow Publishers, Inc.

Library of Congress Cataloging-in-Publication Data

Wingard-Nelson, Rebecca.
 Graphing and probability word problems : no problem! / Rebecca Wingard-Nelson.
    p. cm. — (Math busters word problems)
 Summary: "Presents a step-by-step guide to understanding word problems with graphing and probability"— Provided
by publisher.
 Includes bibliographical references and index.
 ISBN 978-0-7660-3372-6
 1. Word problems (Mathematics)—Juvenile literature. 2. Problem solving—Graphic methods—Juvenile literature.
3. Problem solving—Statistical methods—Juvenile literature. I. Title.
 QA63.W55756 2011
 519.2—dc22
                              2010003281

Printed in the United States of America

062010 Lake Book Manufacturing, Melrose Park, IL

10 9 8 7 6 5 4 3 2 1

To Our Readers: We have done our best to make sure all Internet Addresses in this book were active and appropriate
when we went to press. However, the author and the publisher have no control over and assume no liability for the
material available on those Internet sites or on other Web sites they may link to. Any comments or suggestions can be
sent by e-mail to comments@enslow.com or to the address on the back cover.

♻ Enslow Publishers, Inc., is committed to printing our books on recycled paper. The paper in every book contains
10% to 30% post-consumer waste (PCW). The cover board on the outside of each book contains 100% PCW. Our goal
is to do our part to help young people and the environment too!

Illustration credits: © Comstock/PunchStock, pp. 7, 41; © Digital Vision, p. 9; © Photos.com, p. 45; Shutterstock.com,
pp. 5, 10, 11, 13, 15, 17, 19, 21, 23, 24, 27, 29, 31, 32, 34, 35, 37, 39, 43, 46, 49, 50–51, 53, 54, 57, 58, 60.

Cover illustration: Shutterstock.com

Free Worksheets are available for this book at http://www.enslow.com. Search on the *Math Busters Word Problems*
series name. The publisher will provide access to the worksheets for five years from the book's first publication date.

Contents

When you play cards, or dominoes, or dice games,
you're living in a word problem!
Math is everywhere; you just might not realize it all the time
because math isn't always written as a math problem.

This book will help you understand how data, graphs,
and probability are used in word problems.
The step-by-step method can help students, parents,
teachers, and tutors solve any word problems.
The book can be read from beginning to end
or used to review a specific topic.

① Problem-Solving Tips

How do I start? What do I do if I get stuck?
What if the answer is wrong when I check it?
Word problems are hard for me!

Get Involved!

You can watch a swim meet and see swimmers racing across a pool, but if you want to *learn* to swim, you must get in the water. Solving math problems is not a spectator sport. You may first watch how others solve word problems, but then you need to solve them for yourself, too. Go ahead, jump in!

Practice!

Even the most gifted athlete or musician will tell you that in order to play well, you must practice. The more you practice anything, the better and faster you become at it. The same is true for problem solving. Homework problems and class work are your practice.

Learning Means <u>Not</u> Already Knowing!

If you already know everything, there is nothing left to learn. Every mistake you make is a potential learning experience. When you understand a problem and get the right answer the first time, good for you! When you do NOT understand a problem but figure it out, or you make a mistake and learn from it, AWESOME for you!

Questions, Questions!

Ask smart questions. Whoever is helping you does not know what you don't understand unless you tell them. You must ask a question before you can get an answer.

Ask questions early. Concepts in math build on each other. Today's material is essential to understand tomorrow's.

Don't Give Up!

Stuck on homework? There are many resources for homework help.
• Check a textbook.
• Ask someone who does understand.
• Try looking up sources on the Internet (but don't get distracted).
• Read this book!

Getting frustrated? Take a break.
• Get a snack or a drink of water.
• Move around and get your blood flowing. Then come back and try again.

Stuck on a test? If you do get stuck on a problem, move on to the next one. Solve the problems you understand first. That way you won't miss the problems you do understand because you were stuck on one you didn't. If you have time, go back and try the ones you skipped.

Wrong answer? Check the math; it could be a simple mistake. Try solving the problem another way! There are many problem-solving strategies, and usually more than one of them will work. Don't give up. If you quit, you won't learn anything.

② Problem-Solving Steps

What steps can I take to solve word problems? If I follow the steps, will I be more likely to get a correct answer? Will I have less trouble finding the answer?

Problem-Solving Steps

Step 1: Understand the problem.
Step 2: Make a plan.
Step 3: Follow the plan.
Step 4: Review.

Step 1: Understand the problem.

Read the problem. Read the problem again. This may seem obvious, but this step may be the most important.

Ask yourself questions like:

Do I understand all of the words in the problem?

Can I restate the problem in my own words?

Will a picture or diagram help me understand the problem?

What does the problem ask me to find or show?

What information do I need to solve the problem? Do I have all of the information I need?

Underlining the important information can help you to understand the problem. Read the problem as many times as it takes for you to have a clear sense of what happens in the problem and of what you are asked to find.

Step 2: Make a plan.

There are many ways to solve a math problem. Choosing a good plan becomes easier as you solve more problems. Some plans you may choose are:

Make a list.   *Guess and check.*
Draw a picture.   *Work backward.*
Use logical reasoning.   *Solve a simpler problem.*
Use mental math.   *Use a number line.*
Use a model.   *Use a table.*
Write an equation.   *Read a graph.*

Step 3: Follow the plan.

Now that you understand the problem and have decided how to solve it, you can carry out your plan. Use the plan you have chosen. If it does not work, go back to step 2 and choose a different plan.

Step 4: Review.

Look over the problem and your answer. Does the answer match the question? Does the answer make sense? Is it reasonable? Check the math. What plan worked or did not work? Looking back at what you have done on this problem will help you solve similar problems.

③ Read a Graph

Beach Family Music Downloads

💿 = 100 songs

Jan–Mar	💿 💿 ◗
Apr–June	💿 💿
July–Sept	💿 💿 💿 ◖
Oct–Dec	💿 💿 💿

According to the graph, how many songs did the family download between October and December?

Step 1: Understand the problem.

Read the problem. What does the problem ask you to find?
The number of songs that the Beach family downloaded during October, November, and December.

What information do you need to solve the problem?
The number of symbols on the pictograph for the given months, and the value of each symbol.

Pictographs

A **pictograph** uses symbols to represent data. Each symbol has the same value. To find the measure for an item in a pictograph, you can count the number of symbols and multiply by the value of the symbol.

Step 2: Make a plan.

Count the number of symbols for the time between October and December. Multiply by the value of each symbol, 100 songs.

Step 3: Follow the plan.

There are 3 full symbols for the months of October to December. Multiply.

3 x 100 = 300

The Beach family downloaded 300 songs between October and December.

Step 4: Review.

Does the answer match the question?
Yes. The problem asks for a number of songs.

Check the answer.
**Another way to find the number of songs for the time period is to count by the value of each symbol. The value of each symbol is 100, so count by 100 for each symbol in the October to December row.
Count: 100, 200, 300.
The answer is correct.**

④ Bar Graphs

The newest MP3 player was released in five colors. One store kept track of sales by color for the first month and graphed the data. Which color had the highest sales?

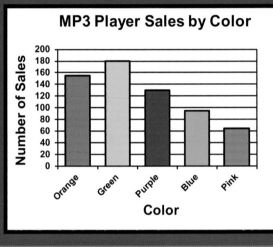

Step 1: Understand the problem.

Read the problem. What does the problem ask you to find?
The color of the MP3 player that sold the most.

What information do you need to solve the problem?
How many players sold in each color.

Do you have all of the information that you need?
The words of the problem do not tell you the number of sales.
The number of sales of each color is given in the graph.

Bar Graphs

A **bar graph** uses horizontal or vertical bars to represent data.
The length of the bar tells you the number it represents.

Step 2: Make a plan.

This problem asks you to compare the number of sales and find the highest, or greatest number. No computations are needed. All you have to do is look at the graph.

Step 3: Follow the plan.

Graph problems that ask you to compare can often be solved just by looking at the graph. The color with the highest bar has the highest sales. Look at the graph.
The green player has the highest bar.

The green MP3 player had the highest sales.

Step 4: Review.

Does the answer match the question?
Yes, the problem asked for a color.

From the information in the graph, could you say that people like the green player more than the pink player?
No. Although it is possible that people like the green player better than the pink one, it cannot be proven from the graph. From the information in the graph you know the sales were higher for the green player than the pink player, but you do not know the reason. It is possible that only a small number of pink players were made, so only a small number could be sold.

How many games had less than 20 points scored?

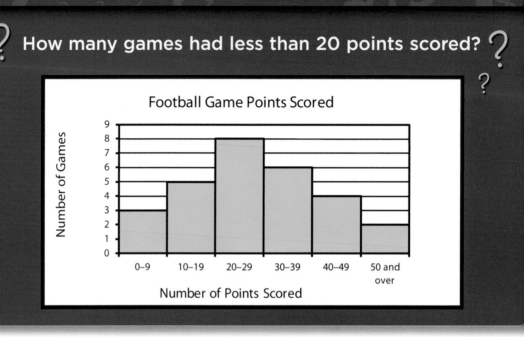

Football Game Points Scored

(Number of Games vs. Number of Points Scored)

Step 1: Understand the problem.

Read the problem. What does the problem ask you to find?
The number of games in which there were less than 20 points scored.

What information do you need to solve the problem?
The number of games in which a given number of points were scored.

Is there extra information?
When a graph is included as part of a word problem, there is probably extra information. You must decide which information you need from the graph.

Step 2: Make a plan.

Each bar in the histogram represents a ten-point range of scores. For example, the first bar represents the number of games with from zero to nine points scored.

Histograms vs. Bar Graphs

The data being graphed in a **histogram** is a group called a range or interval. A bar graph, on the other hand, uses specific numbers instead of ranges. The bars in a histogram touch because all numbers are covered without any gaps. The bars in a bar graph do not touch.

To find the number of games during which less than 20 points were scored, you can add the number of games for each bar where the score was less than 20.

Step 3: Follow the plan.

The first bar tells you that there were 3 games with zero to nine points scored. The second bar tells you that there were 5 games with ten to nineteen points scored. The rest of the bars are for scores of 20 points or higher. Add the number of games from the first two bars.

3 + 5 = 8

There were 8 games with less than 20 points scored.

Step 4: Review.

Does the answer match the question?
Yes, the problem asked for a number of games.

Did the plan work for the problem? **Yes.**

⑥ Line Graphs

Dean's height is measured on his birthday each year. Between which two birthdays did Dean grow the most?

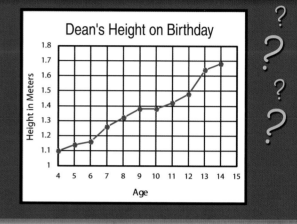

Step 1: Understand the problem.

Read the problem. What does the problem ask you to find?
When Dean grew the most.

What information do you need to solve the problem? Is all of the information that you need in the question?
You need to know Dean's height each year on his birthday. The information in the graph tells you Dean's height on his birthday from ages 4 to 14.

Line Graphs and Change

Line graphs are used to show changes over time. Each point on a line graph represents one item of data. The points are connected by a line.

Lines that go up from left to right show an increase. Lines that go down from left to right show a decrease. The steepness, or slope, of the line shows how much change happened. Steeper lines show faster change. Flatter lines show slower change.

Step 2: Make a plan.

Let's look at the graph to find the answer.

....

Step 3: Follow the plan.

Look at the graph. The line is always going up from left to right. This shows that Dean's height always increased. The problem asks you to find between which two points his height had the greatest change. Find the section of the line that is the steepest (goes up the fastest). It is between his 12th and 13th birthdays.

Dean grew the most between his 12th and 13th birthdays.

....

Step 4: Review.

Does the answer match the question? **Yes. The problem asked for two birthdays.**

Does the answer make sense? **Yes.**

Can you find the answer another way? **Yes. You could find the difference in Dean's height between each birthday using subtraction. It may be difficult to read the exact height Dean was on each birthday using the graph. Try to estimate closely.**

⑦ Circle Graphs

A survey was taken of students' favorite type of fiction book. For this survey, 250 students named mystery as their favorite type of fiction. How many students were surveyed? Explain how you know.

Favorite Type of Fiction

Step 1: Understand the problem.

Read the problem. Is there anything you do not understand? What is a survey? **A survey is a set of questions designed to get information or opinions on a subject. Surveys can be of an entire population or of a smaller sample from a population.**

What does the problem ask you to find?
The number of students that were surveyed. It also asks you to explain your answer.

Is there enough information to solve the problem?
Yes. You know how many students chose mystery as their favorite type of fiction, and the graph shows what part, or fraction, of the total prefer mystery books.

Step 2: Make a plan.

Use the graph to find the fraction of surveyed students who prefer mystery. Use an equation to find the total number of students.

Step 3: Follow the plan.

The graph shows that 1/4 of the students chose mystery as their favorite. The problem tells you that 250 students chose mystery as their favorite. If 1/4 of the whole is 250, you can multiply 250 by 4 to find the whole.

250 × 4 = 1,000

Include an explanation in your answer.

There were 1,000 students surveyed. Since 250 students named mystery as their favorite and they are 1/4 of the survey, then 250 × 4 students were surveyed.

Step 4: Review.

Is there another way you can solve the problem?
Yes. You could set up a proportion.

$$\frac{1}{4} = \frac{250}{?} = \frac{250}{1,000}$$

Circle Graphs

A **circle graph** represents a whole set of data. Each section of the graph represents a part of the data set. Circle graphs are a good way to compare parts of the data to the whole data set.

⑧ Misleading Graphs

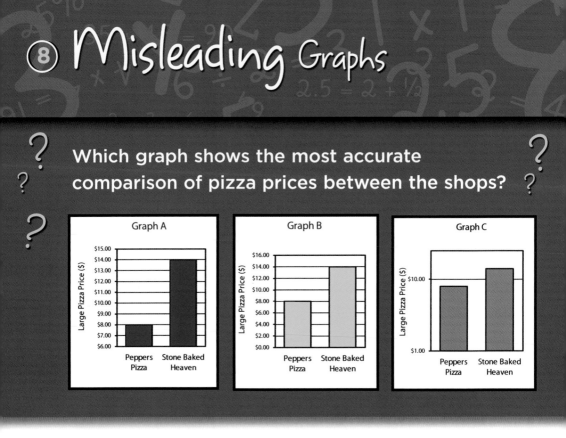

Which graph shows the most accurate comparison of pizza prices between the shops?

Step 1: Understand the problem.

Read the problem. Is there anything you do not understand? What does *accurate comparison* mean? **An accurate comparison is fair or neutral.**
In this problem an accurate comparison would not show any preference over which pizza shop had a better price.

What does the problem ask you to find?
Which of the three graphs is most accurate.

Step 2: Make a plan.

Look at the information in each graph. Compare the way each graph makes the prices appear. Then choose the most accurate.

Step 3: Follow the plan.

Look at the pizza price for each pizza shop on each graph. **Each graph shows a large pizza at Peppers Pizza costs $8.00 and a large pizza at Stone Baked Heaven costs $14.00.**

How does Graph A make the prices appear?
It looks like the pizza costs about 4 times as much at Stone Baked Heaven because the bar is so much taller.

How does Graph B make the prices appear?
It looks like the pizza costs a little less than double at Stone Baked Heaven.

How does Graph C make the prices appear?
It looks like the pizza does not cost very much more at Stone Baked Heaven.

Choose the most accurate graph.

Graph B is the most accurate comparison.

Step 4: Review.

Does the answer match the question?
Yes. The problem asked which graph was most accurate.

How did the other graphs mislead the viewer?
The vertical scale is different in each graph. Graph A started at a price of $6.00 instead of $0.00. Graph C started at $1.00, and only included one interval at $10.00.

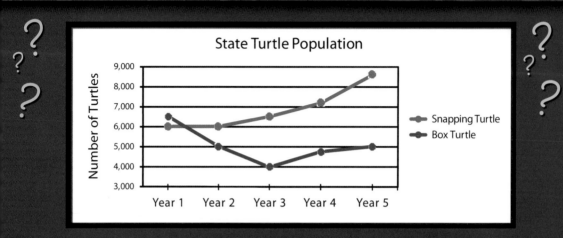

The line graph above shows the turtle population at the end of each year over a five-year period. By the end of the second year, how many more snapping turtles were there than box turtles?

Step 1: Understand the problem.

Read the problem. What does the problem ask you to find?
The difference in the number of snapping turtles and box turtles at the end of the second year.

What information do you need to solve the problem?
The number of snapping turtle and box turtles at the end of the second year.

Step 2: Make a plan.

Use the graph to find the number of each type of turtle at the end of the second year. Write an equation to solve the problem.

Step 3: Follow the plan.

How many snapping turtles were there at the end of the second year?
6,000

How many box turtles were there at the end of the second year?
5,000

Write an equation using words first.

<u>snapping turtles</u> − <u>box turtles</u> = <u>difference</u>

Replace the words with numbers. Then subtract.

6,000 − 5,000 = 1,000

There were 1,000 more snapping turtles than box turtles at the end of the second year.

....

Step 4: Review.

Does the answer match the question?
Yes. The problem asked how many more turtles there were.

Does the answer make sense when you look back at the graph?
**Yes. At the end of the second year, the distance between the two lines is exactly one interval on the vertical scale.
Each interval represents 1,000 turtles.**

Some types of graphs, such as line graphs and bar graphs, can be used to show more than one set of data.

A line graph can show the population change of one type of turtle. A double line graph can show the population change of two types of turtles. The double line graph can be used to compare the changes.

23

? ? ? ?

Katrina made a diagram to show what type of sports her friends like to watch. What sports does Sydney like to watch?

? ? ? ?

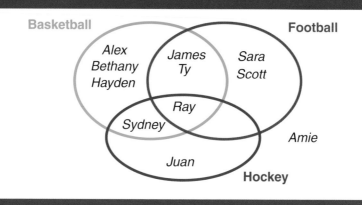

Step 1: Understand the problem.

Read the problem. What does the problem ask you to find?
The type of sports that Sydney likes to watch.

Do you have the information you need to solve the problem? **Yes, it is in the diagram.**

24

Venn Diagrams

Venn diagrams are a way to sort data using intersecting shapes, usually circles or ovals. Each shape is named for the data in it. Each shape has a rule. Data items that follow the rule go inside the shape. Data items that follow more than one rule go in the area where the shapes overlap.

Step 2: Make a plan.

Look at the diagram. Find Sydney's name. Determine which of the shapes her name is inside of, and which sport it stands for.

Step 3: Follow the plan.

Sydney's name is in the section where the blue and green ovals overlap, but not inside the red oval. The blue oval is people who like to watch hockey. The green oval is people who like to watch basketball.

Sydney likes to watch hockey and basketball.

Step 4: Review.

Does the answer match the question?
Yes. The problem asked which sports Sydney likes to watch.

Why is the name Amie not inside any of the ovals?
Amie does not like to watch any of the three sports on the diagram.

Why is this information better shown in a Venn diagram than a bar graph?
A bar graph does not show overlapping information. In a bar graph, you lose the names of the students. For this data, a Venn diagram works nicely because you can see each person, and the overlapping areas make it easy to tell who likes to watch more than one sport.

Naomi asked 40 of her friends how many hours of sleep they normally get on a school night. No one slept less than 4 hours or more than 10 hours. She made a tally chart to keep track of the data.

Number of hours slept			
4			8	卌 卌			
5						9				
6	卌 ||	10	||
7	卌 卌		

Make a frequency table to organize the data.

Step 1: Understand the problem.

Read the problem. Is there anything you do not understand?
A frequency table is a table that tells the frequency, or number of times, an event occurs.

What does the problem ask you to do?
Make a frequency table.

What information do you need to solve the problem?
The data to put in the table.

When you gather information from a survey or observations, you need a way to keep track of the data.

Tallies are an easy way to keep a count of something when you can't keep track in your head.

Tables and charts are used to record and organize data.

Step 2: Make a plan.

The problem tells you the plan. Make a frequency table.

Step 3: Follow the plan.

Set up a table with two columns.

The number of hours slept, (the event) goes in the first column.

Number of hours slept	Frequency
4	1
5	4
6	7
7	10
8	13
9	3
10	2

The second column tells how often each event happened. Count the tally marks. Write each total in the table.

Step 4: Review.

Does the answer match the question?
Yes. The problem said to make a frequency table.

Count the tally for each of the number of hours slept. Are they all correct?
Yes.

The original problem tells you that Naomi asked 40 friends. Add the frequencies. Are there 40 total?
1 + 4 + 7 + 10 + 13 + 3 + 2 = 40
Yes.

⑫ Choose a Graph

Jason took a survey in his study hall about car insurance. Some students didn't drive and didn't need any insurance. Some paid their own insurance. Others had insurance that was paid by someone else. What type of graph is a good way to show the results of the survey?

Step 1: Understand the problem.

Read the problem. Is there anything you do not understand? What does the problem ask you to find?
A type of graph that can be used to display information from a survey.

What information do you need to solve the problem?
The kind of information found by the survey.

Step 2: Make a plan.

Decide what kind of information the survey found. Decide what kind of graph can be used to display the information.

Step 3: Follow the plan.

What kind of information did Jason ask about in his survey?
The information Jason asked about put the students into one of three specific categories.

Which types of graphs show categories of information?
Pictographs, bar graphs, and circle graphs can all show categories of information.

From those types, which graphs work, and which do not?

Pictograph: This could be used. Pictographs are simple and are a good way to show large numbers for each symbol.

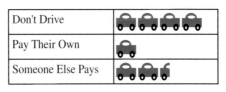

Don't Drive	
Pay Their Own	
Someone Else Pays	

Bar graph: Each category (no insurance, self pay, and someone else pay) can be shown as a bar. Bar graphs make categories easy to compare.

Circle graph: Each category could be shown as a section of the circle. The whole circle represents all of the students in the study hall. Circle graphs make it easy to compare categories, and each category to the whole class.

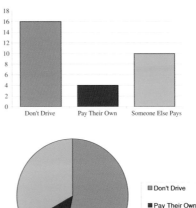

The results of the survey can be displayed well using a pictograph, a bar graph, or a circle graph.

Step 4: Review.

Does the answer match the question?
Yes. The problem asked for types of graphs.

Why can't a line graph or a histogram be used for this information?
A line graph shows how data changes over time. The survey information does not show any changes over time.

A histogram shows numeric data that can be divided into intervals that touch. This survey does not ask for numeric data.

> Of the first 43 United States presidents, 15 were voted into office two or more times. There were 23 presidents who served only one term. There were 5 presidents who were not voted into office. If you were going to make a bar graph to show this data, what values might you use for your vertical scale and interval?

Step 1: Understand the problem.

Read the problem.
What are vertical scale and interval?
Vertical is up and down. The vertical scale is the set of numbers that run up and down the side axis of a graph.

The interval is the amount between each unit on the scale. This scale's interval is 20.

60
40
20
0

What does the problem ask you to find?
A scale and interval for a bar graph showing the number of presidents who were elected for 0, 1, or 2 or more terms.

What information do you need to solve the problem?
The data values that would be graphed.

Step 2: Make a plan.

You are asked to choose a scale and interval, but not to make a graph. Look at the information to choose a scale and interval.

Step 3: Follow the plan.

There are three values to graph as bars. They are 15 (2 or more elections), 23 (1 election), and 5 (0 elections).

The largest value is 23, so the top of the scale must be greater than 23. Numbers ending in 0 or 5 are easy to understand. They are also easy to break into intervals. A good choice for the top of the scale is 25.

The lowest number is 5, so the bottom of the scale must be less than 5. Zero is a good choice for the bottom of the scale.

25 —
20 — It is easy to divide
 25 into intervals
15 — of 5. Two of the
 values, 5 and 15,
10 — end directly on one
 of the intervals.
5 —
0 —

You could choose a scale from 0 to 25, with an interval of 5.

Step 4: Review.

Does the answer match the question?
Yes. The problem asked for a scale and interval.

Is this the only correct answer? **No. You can choose other values for your scale and interval. One other answer could be a scale from 0 to 24, with an interval of 2.**

BALLO
BOX

Make a line graph to display the information given in the table. Use a vertical scale from 20% to 60% with an interval of 4%.

Jack's Free-Throws	
Week	Percent Made
1	26
2	32
3	32
4	34
5	40

Step 1: Understand the problem.

Read the problem. Is there anything you do not understand?

What does the problem ask you to find?
A line graph that shows the same information that is in the table.

Do you have the information you need to make the graph?
All of the information needed is in the table.

Step 2: Make a plan.

The problem tells you the plan. Make a line graph using the given scale and interval.

Step 3: Follow the plan.

Begin your graph with a grid that includes the scale for both axes. The horizontal axis must include weeks 1 through 5. Include a label and values on both axes.
Remember to give your graph a title.

Plot a point for the percent of free-throws Jack made each week. For week 1, follow the line for week 1 up to 26%. Draw a point. Do the same for week 2 through week 5.

Connect the points with lines.

Step 4: Review.

Does the answer match the question?
Yes. The problem asked for a line graph.

How could you have drawn the graph differently to make the data give a different picture?
You could have drawn the horizontal axis with the weeks closer together or farther apart. When the weeks are closer together, the lines are steeper, making it look like there is more change. When they are farther apart, there appears to be less change.

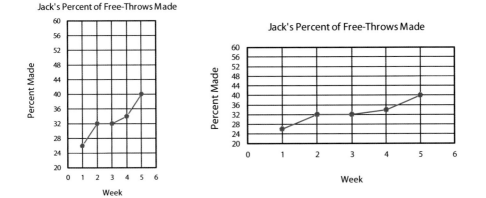

Women's Height and Shoe Size

Shoe Size (y-axis): 4, 5, 6, 7, 8, 9, 10, 11, 12

Height in Inches (x-axis): 52 53 54 55 56 57 58 59 60 61 62 63 64 65 66 67 68 69 70 71 72 73

From the scatterplot shown, what is the approximate height and shoe size of the woman represented by point A?

Step 1: Understand the problem.

Read the problem. Is there anything you do not understand?

What does the problem ask you to find?
An approximate height and shoe size for the woman whose data is graphed at point A.

Do you have all of the information you need to solve the problem?
Yes. The point is on the graph and the graph is clearly labeled.

Step 2: Make a plan.

Find point A and follow the gridline down to find the height and left to find the shoe size.

Scatterplots

A **scatterplot** is used to show data that occurs in numeric pairs. Each point represents two values. One value is found on the horizontal scale and the other on the vertical scale.

Step 3: Follow the plan.

Find point A.

Point A is directly on a point where the gridlines cross. Follow the gridline down to find the height of the person in inches.

The woman is approximately 70 inches tall.

Go back to point A. Follow the gridline left to find the shoe size of the person.

The woman has a shoe size of 9.

The woman represented by point A is about 70 inches tall and wears a size 9 shoe.

Step 4: Review.

Does your answer match the question?
Yes, the problem asked for a height and shoe size.

Why does the problem ask for an approximate height instead of an exact height?
It is impossible to get an exact measurement for the woman's height using a graph. It is also likely that the woman represented by point A is not exactly 70 inches tall. It is more likely she is just over or just under 70 inches tall.

During a 24-hour period with no sleep, students were given a reaction-time test at different times. A faster reaction time scored higher than a slower reaction time. Does the data show a trend? If so, describe the pattern.

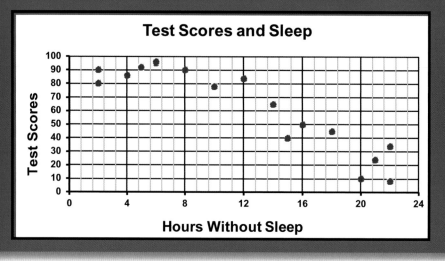

Step 1: Understand the problem.

Read the problem. Is there anything you do not understand? What is a trend? **A trend is a pattern.**

What does the problem ask you to find?
If there is a trend you can see by looking at the data.

Is all of the information that you need in the question?
Yes. The scatterplot shows all of the information.

Step 2: Make a plan.

Look at the scatterplot and decide if a pattern appears in the data.

Step 3: Follow the plan.

One way to see if there is a pattern in the data is to look at the scatterplot from left to right.

Is there a pattern in the data?

Yes. The points appear to get lower on the graph as you go from left to right.

Write this using the information from the graph.

The trend in the data shows that as the number of hours without sleep increases, the test score on the reaction-time test becomes lower.

When two sets of related data increase together, it is called a positive trend. When one set of data increases as the other decreases, it is called a negative trend. Data can have a strong trend, a weak trend, or no trend at all.

Step 4: Review.

Does the answer match the question?
Yes. The problem asked if a trend could be seen in the data, and for a description of the trend.

Does the answer make sense?
Yes, as the students become more tired, you might expect their reaction time to be longer.

⑰ Predictions

? **The scatterplot shows data relating the amount of fat and the number of calories in a serving size of different foods. Make a prediction about the number of calories you might find in a serving of food that contains 15 grams of fat.**

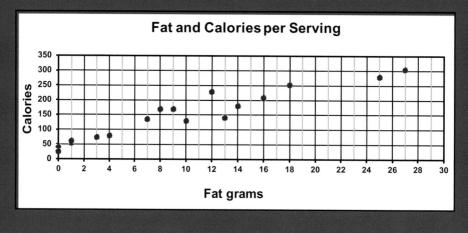

Step 1: Understand the problem.

Read the problem. What does the problem ask you to find?
A prediction of what the number of calories might be in a serving of food with 15 grams of fat.

What information do you need to solve the problem?
The data in the scatterplot about grams of fat and calories.

Step 2: Make a plan.

Look at the scatterplot and see if there are any trends. Use the trend to decide where a serving with 15 grams of fat would most likely fit on the graph.

Step 3: Follow the plan.

There is a trend in the data. The number of calories increases as the number of fat grams increases.

To decide where a serving of food with 15 grams of fat might fit on the graph, you can draw a trend line (a line that follows the trend of the data). The line should have about half of the data points above it, and half below it.

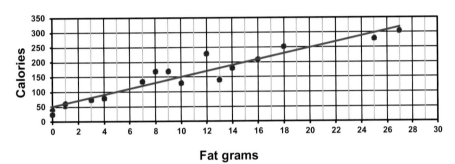

Fat and Calories per Serving

Using the trend line, you can predict about how many calories might be in a serving of food with 15 grams of fat.

The data shows that there could be about 200 calories in a serving of food that contains 15 grams of fat.

Step 4: Review.

Does the answer make sense?
Yes. The foods that contain around 15 grams of fat also have about 200 calories.

? Julie called French horn instructors to find their cost of a weekly lesson. For a one-hour lesson, she was quoted the following costs: $22, $24, $20, $32, $15, and $25. What is the mean cost of a French horn lesson?

Step 1: Understand the problem.

Read the problem. Is there anything you do not understand? What is a mean cost?
In mathematics, the word *mean* **has the same meaning as the word** *average*. **The mean cost, then, is the average cost.**

What does the problem ask you to find?
Find the mean, or average, cost of a French horn lesson.

What information do you need to solve the problem?
The number of costs that were found and the cost of each lesson.

Is all of the information that you need in the question? **Yes.**

Step 2: Make a plan.

Finding a mean can be broken into smaller steps. Let's break the problem into smaller steps.

The mean is the sum of the data values divided by the number of data values.

Step 3: Follow the plan.

To find the mean, first add all of the data values.
Then divide by the number of items in the set.

For this problem, add all of the costs for an hourly lesson.

$22 + $24 + $20 + $32 + $15 + $25 = $138

The problem tells you there are six costs quoted. Count the
number of lesson costs you added to make sure.
Divide the total, $138, by 6.

$138 ÷ 6 = $23

The mean cost of a French horn lesson is $23.

Step 4: Review.

Does the answer match
the question?
**Yes. The problem asked
for the mean cost.**

Does the answer
make sense?
**Yes. Most of the
lesson costs are
close to the mean.
There is one that
is much higher and
one that is much
lower.**

⑲ Median and Mode

Relay runners on the track team recorded their running times for one mile on the first day of practice. What are the median and mode times?

One mile times (min:sec)

9:14	8:50	8:46	10:10	9:16	7:30	5:55	6:40	7:30
8:20	12:05	6:22	7:42	8:01	5:20	6:18	7:02	7:50

Step 1: Understand the problem.

Read the problem. Is there anything you do not understand?

What does the problem ask you to find?
The median and mode of the times for the one-mile run.

What information do you need to solve the problem?
The one-mile time for each runner.

Step 2: Make a plan.

Organize the data by writing them in order from lowest to highest value. Find the median and mode.

Step 3: Follow the plan.

From lowest to highest, the times are:
5:20, 5:55, 6:18, 6:22, 6:40, 7:02, 7:30, 7:30, 7:42, 7:50, 8:01, 8:20, 8:46, 8:50, 9:14, 9:16, 10:10, 12:05

There are 18 recorded times. The median time is the middle value. Since there is an even number of times, the median is halfway between the 9th value (7:42) and 10th value (7:50).

Mean, Median, and Mode

Sometimes a single number is used to describe a set of data. The **mean** of a data set is the average of all of the values.

The **median** of a data set is the middle number when all of the values are listed from lowest to highest. If the set has an even number of values, the median is the value halfway between the two middle numbers.

The **mode** of a data set is the value that occurs most often. If every value occurs the same number of times, there is no mode. If several values occur most often, each is a mode.

Subtract to find the difference between the two values.

7:50 means 7 minutes 50 seconds
7:42 means 7 minutes 42 seconds
_____
                        8 seconds

There is an 8 second difference. To find halfway between, take half of 8 seconds, 4 seconds, and add it to the lower value.

7 minutes 42 seconds + 4 seconds = 7 minutes 46 seconds

The median time is 7:46.

Having the values in order makes it easy to find values that occur more than once. The only value that occurs more than one time is 7:30.

The mode time is 7:30.

Step 4: Review.

Does the answer match the question?
Yes. The problem asked for two things, the median and the mode.

Go back and make sure you have listed all of the data values in the correct order.

⑳ Outliers

Harris has 5 test grades that determine his final grade in math. Harris became ill during one test and only finished half of the problems. His grades are 84, 84, 80, 88, 39.

a. What is the mean test grade?

b. Is there a better description of Harris' knowledge in his math class?

Step 1: Understand the problem.

Read the problem. What does the problem ask you to find? **The mean of Harris' test grades and a better way to describe his knowledge.**

Do you have all of the information you need to solve the problem? **Yes, you know there are 5 grades and you know each grade.**

Step 2: Make a plan.

There are two parts to this problem. Part a: Find the mean. Part b: Think of other ways you can use Harris' test grades to describe what he knows about the math class.

Step 3: Follow the plan.

Part a: Find the sum of the grades. Divide by the number of grades.

84 + 84 + 80 + 88 + 39 = 375
375 ÷ 5 = 75

Harris' mean test grade is a 75.

Part b: Look at the test grades. Put them in order from lowest to highest.

39, 80, 84, 84, 88

Only one test grade is below an 80, but the mean is below an 80. The grade of 39 is an outlier, and affects the mean grade. Since Harris was sick during one of the tests and did not finish, the mean is probably not a good description of how much Harris knows about his math class.

An outlier is a number in a data set that is very different from the rest of the numbers.

Outliers usually affect mean more than they affect the median or mode.

What are the median and mode of the test grades?
The median and mode of the test grades are both an 84.

Both the median and mode of 84 are better descriptions of Harris' knowledge in his math class.

Step 4: Review.

Did you answer the whole question?
Yes. There were two parts to the question. Both were answered.

How much did the outlier affect the mean test grade?
If the outlier is not included, the mean test grade is an 84. The outlier lowered the mean test grade by 9 points.

㉑ Likelihood

Without looking, Breanna draws one card out of a deck of 52 cards. Using the words *likely, unlikely, even chance, certain,* or *impossible,* what is the likelihood that Breanna will draw an ace of hearts?

Step 1: Understand the problem.

Read the problem. Is there anything you do not understand? What do the words *likely, unlikely, certain,* and *impossible* mean?

Likely **means the chances are greater that an event will happen than that it will not happen.** *Unlikely* **means the chances are greater that the event will not happen. A** *certain* **event is one that is going to happen. There is no chance that it will not happen.** *Impossible* **means the event cannot happen.**

What does the problem ask you to find?

The likelihood of Breanna drawing an ace of hearts out of the deck without looking.

What information do you need to solve the problem?

The number of cards in the deck.

Step 2: Make a plan.

Compare the chances of the event happening (drawing an ace of hearts) to the chances of the event not happening.

Step 3: Follow the plan.

There are 52 cards. There is only one ace of hearts in a deck of cards. Breanna has one chance of drawing an ace of hearts. There are 51 cards that are not an ace of hearts. She has 51 chances of not drawing an ace of hearts.

Is it possible for Breanna to draw an ace of hearts? **Yes.**
Is it certain that Breanna will draw an ace of hearts? **No.**
Is Breanna more likely to draw an ace of hearts, or some other card? **Some other card.**

It is unlikely that Breanna will draw an ace of hearts.

Step 4: Review.

Does the answer match the question?
Yes. The problem asked for the likelihood.

Did you use one of the terms listed in the problem?
Yes. The term used was *unlikely***.**

What event matches the term *even chances*?
The term *even chances* **means the event is just as likely to happen as it is to not happen. Half of the cards in a deck are black and half are red. There are even chances of drawing a red or black card.**

On a game show, teens are asked a question. If they answer correctly, they spin this spinner. They win the prize the spinner lands on. What is the sample space for this spinner?

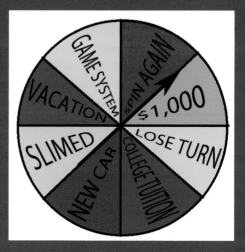

Step 1: Understand the problem.

Read the problem. Is there anything you do not understand? What is a sample space? **A sample space is a list of all of the possible events.**

What does the problem ask you to find?
The sample space of the spinner that is shown.

Is all of the information that you need in the question?
Yes, the spinner is given and labeled.

Step 2: Make a plan.

List all of the possible events the spinner can land on.

Step 3: Follow the plan.

To avoid skipping an event, you can list each one as it appears in a clockwise order. Let's begin with spin again.

The sample space is: spin again, $1,000, lose turn, college tuition, new car, slimed, vacation, game system.

Step 4: Review.

Does the answer match the question?
Yes. The problem asked for the sample space.

Check to make sure you did not miss any outcomes.
Count the number of regions on the spinner. **There are 8.**
Count the number of outcomes in the sample space.
There are 8.

㉓ Probability

Jeri's bag of jelly beans has 4 yellow, 2 pink, 5 red, 1 green, and 4 purple beans in it. If she reaches in and randomly chooses a jelly bean, what is the probability that it is purple?

Step 1: Understand the problem.

Read the problem. What does the problem ask you to find?
The probability that a randomly chosen jelly bean will be purple.

What information do you need to solve the problem?
The total number of jelly beans and the number that are purple.

Step 2: Make a plan.

Find the total number of jelly beans using addition. Write a fraction to show the probability of randomly choosing a purple jelly bean.

Probability

Probability is a way to describe the likelihood of an event using a number from 0 through 1. A probability of 0 means the event is impossible. A probability of 1 means the event is certain. Probabilities can be written as fractions, decimals, or percents.

Step 3: Follow the plan.

You can write a probability as a fraction. Put the number of ways a given event can happen in the numerator (top number). The number of possible outcomes goes in the denominator (bottom number).

$$probability = \frac{\textbf{ways an event can happen}}{\textbf{total possible outcomes}}$$

There are four purple jelly beans left in the bag. Jeri can choose a purple four ways.

Find the total number of jelly beans using addition.

4 yellow + 2 pink + 5 red + 1 green + 4 purple = 16 total

Substitute the numbers into the probability fraction.

$$probability = \frac{\textbf{ways an event can happen}}{\textbf{total possible outcomes}} = \frac{4}{16} = \frac{1}{4}$$

The probability of Jeri choosing a purple jelly bean is 1/4.

Step 4: Review.

Does the answer match the question?
Yes. The problem asks for a probability.

Is there another way to solve this problem?
Yes. You could write the probability as a decimal (1/4 = 0.25), or as a percent (1/4 = 25%).

The probability that a traffic light is red is 0.45.
What is the probability that the light is not red?
The probability that the same light is yellow is 0.1.
What is the probability that the light is green?

Step 1: Understand the problem.

Read the problem. What does the problem ask you to find?
There are two questions. One asks for the probability of the traffic light not being red. The other asks for the probability of the light being green.

Is all of the information that you need in the question?
Yes, the probabilities for a red light and a yellow light are given.

Step 2: Make a plan.

Write an equation to find each part of the answer.

Step 3: Follow the plan.

The total probability of all of the possible events is 1.
To find the probability of an event not happening, subtract the probability of the event from the total probability, 1.

$$\underline{\text{total probability}} - \underline{\begin{array}{c}\text{probability of} \\ \text{red light}\end{array}} = \underline{\text{probability of not red light}}$$

$$1 \qquad - \qquad 0.45 \quad = \qquad 0.55$$

The probability that the traffic light is not red is 0.55.

The second part of the problem asks you for the probability of a green light. You can add and subtract probabilities just like other fractions, decimals, and percents. One way to solve this

Complement

The **complement** of an event is the outcome of an event NOT happening. The probability of the complement of an event is the probability that the event will not happen.

problem is to write an addition equation showing that the probabilities for each color light have a sum of one.

probability of: <u>red light</u> + <u>yellow light</u> + <u>green light</u> = 1

Substitute the numbers you know. Then add.

0.45 + 0.1 + green light = 1
0.55 + green light = 1

Subtract to find the answer.

probability of a green light =
1 — 0.55 = 0.45

The probability of a green light is 0.45.

The odds of an event happening is the ratio of the event to the complement of the event.

For example, if one in ten students has green eyes, the probability of having green eyes is 1 out of 10. The odds of a student having green eyes is 1 to 9.

Step 4: Review.

Check the math.
The sum of the probabilities for the events is always 1.
probability of: red light + yellow light + green light = 1
0.45 + 0.1 + 0.45 = 1

The hot dog vendor in the park offers two kinds of hot dogs: beef and spicy. You can get the hot dog on a white bun or a honey bun. You can have the hot dog plain, with chili, or with sauerkraut. How many combinations of hot dog, bun, and topping are possible?

Step 1: Understand the problem.

Read the problem. What does the problem ask you to find?
The number of combinations of hot dog, bun, and topping you can make.

Do you have all of the information you need to solve the problem?
Yes. You know the kinds of hot dog available, kinds of bun available, and kinds of toppings available.

Step 2: Make a plan.

Let's make a tree diagram to find all of the combinations, then count them.

Step 3: Follow the plan.

A tree diagram is a way to make an organized list.

Begin with the two types of hot dog. Each can be put on either kind of bun. Each of those combinations can have one of the toppings. The possible combinations can be listed on the right.

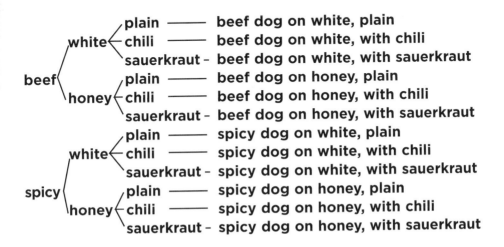

		plain —	beef dog on white, plain
	white	chili —	beef dog on white, with chili
		sauerkraut –	beef dog on white, with sauerkraut
beef		plain —	beef dog on honey, plain
	honey	chili —	beef dog on honey, with chili
		sauerkraut –	beef dog on honey, with sauerkraut
		plain —	spicy dog on white, plain
	white	chili —	spicy dog on white, with chili
		sauerkraut –	spicy dog on white, with sauerkraut
spicy		plain —	spicy dog on honey, plain
	honey	chili —	spicy dog on honey, with chili
		sauerkraut –	spicy dog on honey, with sauerkraut

There are 12 possible combinations.

Step 4: Review.

Does the answer match the question?
Yes. The problem asked for the number of possible combinations.

In a probability problem, what would the list of different combinations be called? **The sample space, with each combination as an event.**

㉖ The Counting Principle

The Conservation Club is choosing one boy and one girl to represent them at a state conference. There are 6 girls and 4 boys who would like to go. How many combinations of a girl and boy are possible?

Step 1: Understand the problem.

Read the problem. What does the problem ask you to find? **The number of combinations of one boy and one girl.**

Do you have all of the information you need to solve the problem? **Yes, you know there are 6 girls and 4 boys.**

Step 2: Make a plan.

Use multiplication to find the number of combinations.

Step 3: Follow the plan.

You know there are six girls. Each of the six girls could go to the conference with any one of the four boys. Multiply to find the number of possible combinations.

$6 \times 4 = 24$

There are 24 possible combinations of one girl and one boy.

Step 4: Review.

Does the answer match the question?
Yes. The question asked for the number of possible combinations of a boy and a girl.

Is there another way you can find the answer?
Yes. You could use a tree diagram, or organized list, with this list of outcomes:

girl 1, boy 1	girl 2, boy 1	girl 3, boy 1
girl 1, boy 2	girl 2, boy 2	girl 3, boy 2
girl 1, boy 3	girl 2, boy 3	girl 3, boy 3
girl 1, boy 4	girl 2, boy 4	girl 3, boy 4
girl 4, boy 1	girl 5, boy 1	girl 6, boy 1
girl 4, boy 2	girl 5, boy 2	girl 6, boy 2
girl 4, boy 3	girl 5, boy 3	girl 6, boy 3
girl 4, boy 4	girl 5, boy 4	girl 6, boy 4

Then count the outcomes. There are 24.

Compound Events

The probability that a child is a girl is 1/2.
What is the probability of all 3 children in
a family being girls?

Step 1: Understand the problem.

Read the problem. Is there anything you do not understand?

What does the problem ask you to find?
The probability that a family with 3 children will have all girls.

Do you have all of the information you need to solve the problem?
Yes. You know the probability of each child being a girl.

Step 2: Make a plan.

Find the number of outcomes using a tree diagram. Write the probability of all three children being girls as a fraction.

Step 3: Follow the plan.

Draw a tree diagram.

```
          girl ┌ girl — girl, girl, girl
girl ┌         └ boy — girl, girl, boy
     │
     └    boy ┌ girl — girl, boy, girl
              └ boy — girl, boy, boy

          girl ┌ girl — boy, girl, girl
boy ┌          └ boy — boy, girl, boy
    │
    └     boy ┌ girl — boy, boy, girl
              └ boy — boy, boy, boy
```

> A compound event is the combination of two or more single events. In this problem, each child being a girl is a single event. All three children being girls is a compound event.

There are 8 outcomes.
Only one of the outcomes is three girls.

The probability of all 3 children in a family being girls is 1/8.

Step 4: Review.

Does your answer match the problem?
Yes. The problem asked for a probability.

Is there another way you can solve the problem?
Yes. You can find the probability of two or more combined events by multiplying the probabiltiy of each event. In this problem, the probabilty of each event is the same. For three children, multiply the probability of a girl three times.

$1/2 \times 1/2 \times 1/2 = 1/8$

Xavier was trying to find what kind of music students listen to while they study. He surveyed 100 students. Of these students, 55 said rock music, 20 said country, 15 said hip-hop, and 10 said jazz. From these results, if there are 620 students in Xavier's school, how many would you expect to say jazz?

Step 1: Understand the problem.

Read the problem.
What does the problem ask you to find?
The number of students you would expect to say jazz as the music they like to listen to while they study.

Do you have all of the information you need to solve the problem?
Yes. You know how many students from the survey chose jazz.

Step 2: Make a plan.

Use the survey data to predict.

Samples

When you do an experiment to get an idea about probability, it is called **sampling**. Surveys are one form of sampling. The probability obtained from samples is called **experimental probability**. Experimental probability can be misleading if you do not have enough samples. For example, if you flipped a coin four times, and three of the times it was heads showing, the experiment might lead you to believe the probability of heads is 0.75. If you continue to flip the coin, the experimental probability should become closer to the actual probability of 0.5.

Step 3: Follow the plan.

The survey data tells you that out of the 100 students surveyed, 10 said jazz. The experimental probability of a student choosing jazz is 10/100, or 10%.

If the probability of a student saying jazz is 10%, and there are 620 students, you can multiply to predict the total number of students who would say jazz.

620 students × 10% = 62 students

You would expect 62 students to say jazz is the music they like to listen to while studying.

Step 4: Review.

Does the answer match the question?
Yes. The problem asked for a prediction.

How accurate is Xavier's data?
You need more information to know. If Xavier only surveyed his friends, they might have a higher preference for a certain style of music. Or if he only surveyed athletes, or musicians, the data might not be a good representation of the whole school.

How could the data be more accurate?
Survey a larger group of people.

61

Further Reading

Books

Lerner, Marcia, and Doug McMullen. *Math Smart Junior.* New York.: Random House, 2008.

Long, Lynette. *Great Graphs and Sensational Statistics.* Hoboken, N.J.: Wiley, 2004.

More math help from Rebecca Wingard-Nelson:

Wingard-Nelson, Rebecca. *Data, Graphing, and Statistics.* Berkeley Heights, N.J.: Enslow Publishers, Inc., 2004.

Internet Addresses

Glosser, Gisele. *Math Goodies.* "Probability." © 1999–2009. <http://www.mathgoodies.com/lessons/vol6/intro_probability.html>

Kids' Zone. "Create a Graph." © 2010. <http://www.nces.ed.gov/nceskids/createagraph/default.aspx>

Math Is Fun. "Using and Handling Data." © 2009. <http://www.mathsisfun.com/data/>

Math League Press. "Using Data and Statistics." © 1997–2006. <http://mathleague.com/help/data/data.htm>

Index